Baltimore & Ohio
MAGNIFICENT 2-8-8-4 EM-1 ARTICULATED LOCOMOTIVE

By Thomas W. Dixon, Jr. & Bob Withers

TLC Publishing, Inc. 2007

TABLE OF CONTENTS

Foreword..*iii*

Introduction..*iv*

    Pioneer and Experimenter...*iv*

    A New Concept...*iv*

    Finally, New Thinking...*v*

    Appearance..*viii*

SECTION ONE: Mallets and Mountains..1

SECTION TWO: The Cumberland Division..12

SECTION THREE: The Diesel-Driven Dispersal..43

SECTION FOUR: Then Cometh the End...68

International Standard Book Number: 0-939487-83-7

Design & Layout by
Megan Johnson
Johnson2Design
Rustburg, VA

Printed in USA
by McClain Printing Company, Parsons, WV

FOREWORD

I have called myself a compiler than an author for this small book, mainly because I feel that I am not qualified to do the work as a contribution to genuine B&O history. However, my fellow compiler, Bob Withers, is a B&O expert, and his work has helped this be a much better book than it could have been otherwise.

This book largely is a collection of very nice photos, many of which were taken by Bruce D. Fales and supplied to me through the good offices of Jay Williams. We have arranged an album that we hope will show these magnificent locomotives for what they were — transportation giants.

I have studied and written about the Chesapeake & Ohio Railway for almost 40 years. Of course, that company's motive power stable epitomized the big locomotive. And, more than that, C&O came to be understood as a carrier that purchased not only the biggest, but also the most modern. It wasn't that innovative, though, until the very end of steam.

B&O was the opposite, in that while it didn't have the money to buy the biggest and the best, it was quite innovative and willing to experiment with steam motive power.

By happenstance of World War II, B&O acquired its great modern EM-1 2-8-8-4 simple articulated locomotives from Baldwin Locomotive Works of Philadelphia. They were every bit the match for the best that Lima and the other superpower builders could produce — although Lima gets most of the credit for the superpower phenomenon. Whether or not the EM-1's qualified as superpower probably is debatable, but I think they met most of the requirements. Had it not been for wartime restrictions imposed by the War Production Board, they would never have been built — and B&O would have dieselized much sooner than it did.

From their arrival during the final, peak years of the war down to their last operating days in 1957, they did superb work no matter what jobs they were assigned. It is a pleasure to be a part of memorializing in print this great class of locomotives.

Thomas W. Dixon Jr.
Lynchburg, Va.
December 2007

INTRODUCTION

This book will argue that the Class EM-1 2-8-8-4 simple articulated locomotive represents the high point in the Baltimore & Ohio Railroad Company's steam power development — and was the carrier's only "modern" steamer. Many also will argue that it was among the company's best-looking locomotives. Of course, beauty is in the eye of the beholder, and B&O certainly had many well-proportioned and classic locomotives — both during the final 50 years of steam operation and in the early years, too, since the company spanned the entire history of railroad locomotive development from the first day to the last.

This book is first and foremost a picture album of these magnificent machines, which came during World War II and stayed on for barely past a decade, handling the heaviest forms of work before finally being displaced by the all-conquering diesel.

Pioneer and Experimenter

B&O was America's first common-carrier railroad, having been chartered in 1827. During most of the 19th century, the company pioneered the development and refinement of railroad technology — including the design and enlargement of steam engines. But by the 1920s, the road had fallen behind its competitors, and it never was to be counted among the lines that bought into the modern "superpower" concept of steam locomotive design originated by Lima Locomotive Works and, later, by Baldwin and American.

However, B&O did many great experiments in the field, including development of the first compound articulated Mallet, the sleek 4-4-4-4 water-tube *Lady Baltimore* and other water-tube types, and the European-looking *Lord Baltimore*. But, the fact is, none of these came into common use on B&O or any other road. Because of a lack of investment capital, B&O tended to operate during most of the first half of the 20th century with small locomotives

and seldom made large purchases of new engines after 1927.

B&O recognized early on the value of the diesel-electric locomotive. It experimented first with a tiny switcher for the compact freight yard in Manhattan in 1925. Then, it purchased several units for passenger service beginning a decade later. In 1942, the company purchased its first road freight diesels and soon the management was so pleased with the internal combustion concept in both passenger and freight applications that it was ready for more. But by then, the United States government had restricted the types of power railroads could buy because of the exigencies of war. For this reason, when it became necessary to purchase new power, B&O was forced to choose steam. The great EM-1's were the result of that choice.

A New Concept

Invented by Frenchman Anatole Mallet in 1876, the articulated locomotive was equipped with two independent sets of cylinders and driving wheels beneath an elongated boiler. The forward of these two "engines" was attached to the boiler only at its rear end so it could swivel, while the second engine was attached rigidly. As the locomotive negotiated curves, the front engine turned to the right or left independently of the boiler.

The first articulated types also were "compounds," meaning their steam was used twice. First, high-pressure steam from the boiler was fed into the rear cylinders and used to propel the driving rods. The steam then was exhausted to be used again in the front set of cylinders — which had to be much larger because the once-used steam's pressure was now lower and its volume much expanded — and finally exhausted into the atmosphere through the stack. Compounding was first applied to non-articulated locomotives, but it was admirably suited for the articulated design.

So B&O placed the first compound articulated locomotive in America in service in 1904 with its 0-6-6-0 No. 2400, which crews affectionately nicknamed "Old Maude" after a balky comic-strip mule of the period. After the strange new contraption was exhibited at that year's Louisiana Purchase Exposition in St. Louis, it was placed in helper service on B&O's Sand Patch Grade in Pennsylvania.

In 1911, B&O tried another type of Mallet, this time crafting an odd and never-repeated 2-6-8-0 wheel arrangement by adding a front section to an existing 2-8-0. The experiment seemed to recognize that a locomotive without a leading truck was unsuitable for road service.

In 1911-1913, B&O bought its first full class of articulated locomotives — but this time ordered 30 0-8-8-0's, still not applying a leading truck. They were generally unsatisfactory, but some of them hung around for decades. More Mallets followed, complete with leading trucks — 30 2-8-8-0's in 1916, 30 more in 1917, and still 26 more in 1919-20. In 1922, the company bought 16 2-8-8-2's secondhand from the Seaboard Air Line Railroad, and when it built a single 2-6-6-0 and a similar 2-6-6-2 in 1930, completed the company's pre-World War II roster of Mallets.

It was with the first 20 EM-1's, built in 1944, that B&O received its first new simple articulateds — "simple" because all four cylinders used high-pressure steam from the boiler. Several older engines had been converted in previous years because the design provided a great deal more power. But it also required larger fireboxes and free-steaming boilers in order to provide enough high-pressure steam. The trade-off was acceptable, though, and more "simples" followed — 10 more EM-1's in 1945 and 10 secondhand 2-6-6-4's from the Seaboard in 1947. That purchase completed B&O's all-time Mallet roster.

B&O's articulated locomotives generally were used in slow drag service, both as road engines and helpers on the line's heaviest grades. The more modern simples types that were being built for other roads also were being used for fast freight service — but for a long time, B&O was satisfied with the slower movements and saw no need to pursue the superpower concept. That is, until the EM-1 came along.

Finally, New Thinking

The B&O Class EM-1 was a simple articulated steam locomotive with a 2-8-8-4 wheel arrangement. That type of locomotive was first built for the Northern Pacific Railway in 1928, and was generally known as the "Yellowstone" type, from the name adopted by the NP. On that road, the trailing truck was expanded from two to four wheels to support the larger firebox required to burn the low-volatile lignite coal that was plentiful in that region.

Afterward, the design also was built for carriers using bituminous coal. Commonly, these engines had 63-inch drivers and simple cylinders. The Southern Pacific was fond of this type, but their designers turned them around to become that company's fabled "cab-forward" types to keep their choking exhausts away from crews running through tunnels.

In the Eastern United States, one of the most successful simple articulated locomotives was the Chesapeake & Ohio's 2-8-8-2's built in 1923-24. They were credited with establishing the simple articulated type as a standard road engine.

B&O's mechanical department, always the experimenter, probably took note of all this. Of course, by the World War II era, diesels — highlighted by EMD's FT model road freight units — were all the rage, but a massive infusion of diesel power to support the ballooning war traffic was impossible because of limitations on new locomotive development and purchases imposed by the War Production Board.

So, given the circumstances, B&O's decision to buy new 2-8-8-4's during the peak years of the war was a natural one. The line had good experience with Mallets handling slow, heavy trains, and the large simple articulated design offered better capability to do this coupled with the potential bonus of providing faster mixed freight service.

The first 20 EM-1's, constructed in 1944, were numbered 7600-7619. The additional 10 engines, built between May and August 1945 with basically the same specifications, were numbered 7620-7629.

Those specifications follow:

Steam pressure	235 pounds per square inch
Boiler diameter, first ring, inside	94 $\frac{1}{8}$ inches
Firebox length and width	228 by 96 inches
Grate length	177 inches
Grate area	117.5 square feet
Combustion chamber length	90 inches
Tubes, number and diameter	63, 2¼ inches
Flues, number and diameter	177, 4 inches
Length over tube sheets	20 feet, 6 inches
Cylinder diameter and stroke	24 by 32 inches
Cylinder centers	93 inches
Driver diameter	64 inches
Pony wheel diameter	33 inches
Trailing wheel diameter	42 inches
Rated tractive force	115,000 pounds
Valve gear	Walschaerts
Piston valve diameter	12 inches
Maximum piston travel	7 inches
Cut-off in full gear	85.3 percent
Feedwater heater	Worthington
Superheater	Type E
Height, rail to top of stack	15 feet, 11 inches
Height, rail to center of boiler	10 feet, 8 inches
Width	10 feet, 10 ⅝ inches
Length, locomotive and tender	125 feet, 9 ⅝ inches
Wheelbase, drivers, each engine	16 feet, 9 inches
Wheelbase, drivers, both engines	44 feet, 3 inches
Wheelbase, total locomotive	65 feet, 2 inches
Wheelbase, locomotive and tender	112 feet, 6 inches
Length of turntable required	115 feet
Weight on front truck	50,700 pounds
Weight on drivers	485,000 pounds
Weight on drivers as percent of engine weight	77.2 percent
Factor of adhesion	4.22
Weight on front truck	50,700 pounds
Weight on drivers	485,000 pounds
Weight on trailing truck	93,000 pounds
Weight, total locomotive	628,700 pounds
Weight, fully loaded tender	382,000 pounds
Weight, locomotive and tender	1,010,700 pounds
Tender style	Rectangular, welded
Tender coal capacity	25 tons
Tender water capacity	22,000 gallons

The EM-1's were equipped with power reverses, stokers, firebox siphons and lateral cushioning devices on the front driver axle of each engine and the leading trailing truck axle. They had roller bearings on all wheels; with their cylinder cocks open, three men could push one on level track — earning them a reputation for being "yard creepers."

Except for some minor staybolt problems, they were virtually perfect. After inspecting the first one that was delivered, B&O President Roy B. White turned to A.K. Galloway, general superintendent motive power and equipment, and said, "Well, I must say, they have everything."

One of the advantages of the articulated design was the relatively light weight per driving wheel axle, which for the EM-1 was 60,625 pounds. Another was the short rigid wheelbase of 16 feet, 9 inches, because of the division of the 16 drivers into two engines of eight wheels apiece — allowing movement through curves as sharp as 18 degrees.

The straight-top boiler, with a 96⅛ inch diameter at the front and a length, including the smokebox, of 59 feet, 5 inches, was assembled with carbon steel plates 1 inch and 1 1/32 inch thick, with three rings in the barrel. The steam dome, placed on the second ring, had a 36-inch diameter and was 9 inches high. The boiler itself was triple-riveted on the circumferential seams, while the longitudinal seams were closed with sawtooth weld strips. The longitudinal seams, on the first and second rings, were welded for 16 inches at each end while the third ring was welded throughout its length.

The large firebox, with its grate area of 117.5 square feet, and the 90-inch-long combustion chamber in front of it, provided an overall length from the fire door to the back tube sheet of 26 feet, 6 inches. Total firebox volume was 892 cubic feet. Five Nicholson thermic siphons — three in the firebox and two in the combustion chamber — provided increased heating area. The siphons were simply water legs through which water could circulate and be heated in addition to the surface area that surrounded the firebox and crown sheet. The combustion chamber merely added space ahead of the grates where the gases could be heated further before entering the tubes.

The 177 4-inch flues were 20 feet, 6 inches, long, and the minimum gas area through the flues and tubes was 11.21 square feet.

The EM-1 was equipped with a Standard type HT-M stoker, which fired through the firebox door. The ash pan had three hoppers, which were operated from the ground. The boiler was fed by a 12,500-gallon Ohio type injector. A Worthington model 6SA feedwater heater, which received exhaust from all four cylinders, was installed in the smokebox — with its cold-water pump mounted in the left rear and its hot-water pump on the smokebox front. A Cyclone front-end arrangement was used.

Boiler accessories included a flue blower and an Ohio low-water alarm. The air compressors and the blower were operated by superheated steam. The three Coale safety valves, each 4 inches in diameter, were inserted into the boiler just behind the steam dome.

The EM-1's chassis was composed of two bed castings with integral cylinders provided by General Steel Casting Corporation. The radius bar for the articulation joint was cast in one piece with the front bed so that its flexibility was provided in only the horizontal plane. The load was transferred to the truck by two leaf springs. The boiler's weight was transferred through a single waist bearer placed under the smokebox above the second driving axle. A centering spring was installed between the second and third set of drivers.

The steam distribution system was controlled by 12-inch B&O standard piston valves that had a steam lap of 1¼ inches, 7 inches of travel, a lead of 3/16 inch and a maximum cutoff of 85.3 percent in full gear. Manufactured from forged steel and separate shoes, the pistons were equipped with B&O standard packing rings and crossheads. The Alco type H power reverse was attached to the boiler in front of the right rear cylinder. Needle bearings were used in the valve gear connections.

The main and side rods were made of tempered carbon steel, the side rods having a rectangular section. Floating bushings were used on the main and side rods, connecting them to the main pins; steel spacing rings were placed on the pins between the side and main rod studs. All driving axles were equipped with Timken roller bearings and the driving wheels featured boxpok centers. Alco lateral motion devices were applied to the first pair of drivers on each engine and the leading trailing truck axle was equipped with a Timken lateral motion device.

The main drivers were cross-balanced; of the total reciprocating weight of 3,050 pounds, 912 pounds was balanced — leaving an unbalanced portion of 3.4 percent per 1,000 pounds of total locomotive weight. The overbalance was distributed equally to the front, intermediate and rear wheels, with no overbalance on the main wheels. The dynamic augment at diameter speed was 7,800 pounds.

(Dynamic augment — commonly referred to as "pounding," referred to the force produced by the centrifugal action of a portion of the driving wheel counterbalance weight added to oppose the thrust of the reciprocating parts and acting in a direction perpendicular to them. This force, when exerted downward, increased the wheel's pressure on the rail, and when acting upward tended to lift the wheel off the rail. So the tremendous weight exerted by the throw of those reciprocating parts literally lifted the locomotive's weight up and down on the rail at every stroke. The problem caused roadbeds to deteriorate so rapidly in the steam era that constant maintenance was required. Steam's demise also brought the end of dynamic augment, resulting in much easier roadbed maintenance in the diesel era.)

External piping to and from the cylinders was placed left and right, carrying live steam from the superheater header in the smokebox to the rear cylinders. Here, each pipe was divided, each branch leading to the corresponding steam chest. Other pipe branches joined at the center of the locomotive, leading steam to the front cylinders through a single ball-jointed pipe. The rear cylinders' exhaust was carried to the smokebox through outside pipes, while that from the front cylinders passed through a central pipe fitted with a ball joint at each end and an intermediate slip joint.

The EM-1's were equipped with two 2,500-pound sandboxes. Sand was delivered at the front and rear of the main drivers and ahead of the front drivers of each engine. A rail-washing device was placed under the cab to clear the used sand from the rail.

Two Westinghouse cross-compound air compressors were mounted low on the forward end of the bed. Westinghouse also manufactured the brake equipment.

Two forced-feed lubricators were placed on each engine, operated from combination levers. The left-side lubricators served the cylinders and valves; those on the right lubricated the chassis. Flange lubrication was supplied to the leading drive wheels on each engine.

The locomotives featured extremely large cabs. They were of welded steel construction, 8 feet 5 inches long by 10 feet 4 inches wide. They had one seat on the right side for the engineer and two seats on the left for the fireman and head brakeman. Foot-warmers were provided for each seat and non-shattering glass was installed in the windows.

The EM-1 tender was carried on two Buckeye six-wheel trucks with class brakes. The tender's frame, supplied by General Steel Castings Corporation, was of the cast-steel, water-bottom type with a capacity of 22,000 gallons of water and 25 tons of coal. The tank, designed by Baldwin, was welded throughout. The tenders were equipped with either Timken or SKF roller bearings.

Appearance

Steam locomotive fans almost universally agree that the EM-1's were good-looking. They succeeded in combining their massive bulk and myriads of appliances, pipes and devices into an integrated whole that simply exuded the aura of power. The clean smokebox front, highlighted by the B&O Capitol dome emblem on the small smokebox door, also gave them a pleasing face.

As viewed from the front, they had a slatted pilot, with six slats on each side of the coupler, an air after-cooler behind a screen and pumps mounted behind the shields, all mounted on the pilot deck with the headlight. That latter feature was standard for all B&O articulateds, a necessary design so the headlight would track with the front engine rather than the boiler. The bell was mounted at the top of the smokebox, with the rectangular number plate under it.

Viewed from the side or ¾ angle, the boiler was fairly free of appliances above the running board, with air reservoirs mounted below. Steam piping to and from the cylinders was partially visible between the running boards and the drivers. The boxpok driver center somehow added to the appearance of power. Two stacks, one each for the front and rear engine's exhaust, were affixed to the top of the smokebox. The two large sandboxes — sometimes called sand domes — were positioned fore and aft of the steam dome. The sand pipes were concealed under the boiler jacket and the whistle was mounted on the side of the steam dome. The large-capacity tender fit the locomotive's dimensions well.

Section One:
MALLETS AND MOUNTAINS

From the day the first EM-1 was delivered to the Cumberland, Md., shop in February 1944, B&O was as proud of the class as an Eagle Scout's father. This section shows how eager the railroad, the locomotive's builder, and railfans alike were to show off the carrier's newest and grandest steam power.

In the 1940s and early '50s, B&O's public relations department was ever ready to extol the virtues of its equipment. The office issued a series of sheets describing a certain locomotive or car, an illustration of it, a scale drawing (usually 1 inch equals 1 foot), and some of its salient aspects. Reproduced on the following pages are the sheets prepared for the EM-1 in 1946 as part of this series.

TLC Publishing Inc. Collection

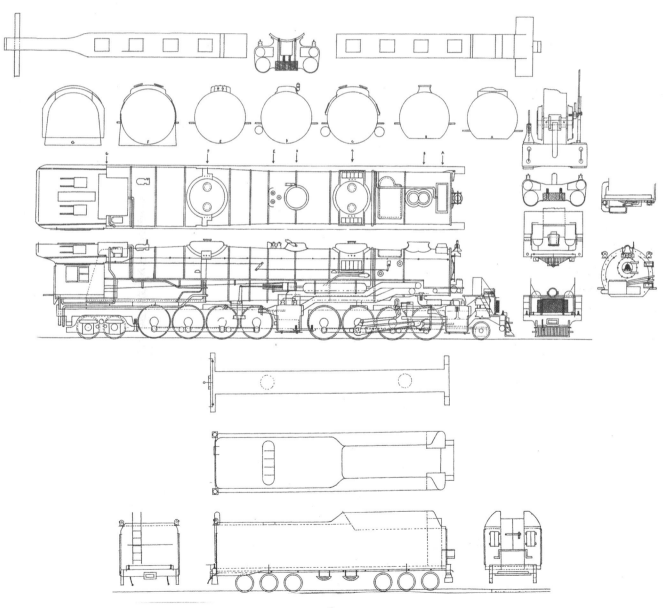

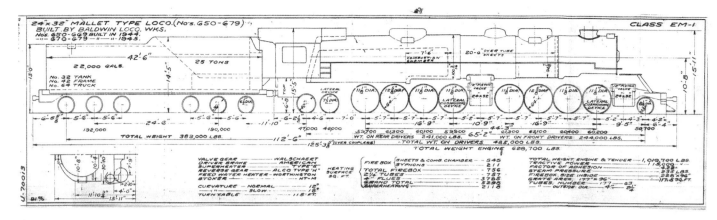

This is the official B&O mechanical department diagram for the EM-1, updated to 1957 — just before the class was retired at the end of steam operations.

TLC Publishing Inc. Collection

Baldwin chose engine 7628 to represent the second batch of EM-1's, which was completed in August 1945. It is seen here, glistening in the sun on its first day out of the shop in a ¾ view. The second lot of EM-1's were, for all practical purposes, identical to their older sisters.

Baldwin Locomotive Works/TLC Publishing Inc. Collection

This nearly broadside builder's view of the 7600 gives a good impression of the 1944 locomotive's size and almost sleek appearance. This well-groomed aura was enhanced by the relatively clean boiler jacket, with even the sand pipes concealed. The standard small B&O lettering seems tiny on the giant tender.

Baldwin Locomotive Works/TLC Publishing Inc. Collection

The head-on smokebox view of the 7628 is indeed impressive, showing the low-mounted headlight, high bell and number plate, and the classy B&O Capitol dome emblem on the small round smokebox door. For such a massive locomotive, she had a pleasing face.

TLC Publishing Inc. Collection

This view of an EM-1's backhead is typical of the appearance of a modern steam locomotive.

Baldwin Locomotives, third quarter 1946/TLC Publishing Inc. Collection

This slightly elevated view offers another perspective of the EM-1's mass. Note that the sand piping running down from the 7603's forward sandbox, although still sheathed under the jacket, has a different appearance than that on the builder's photos of the 7600 and the 7628 shown earlier. Also note the overfire jets on the side of the firebox.

TLC Publishing Inc. Collection

Although most often pictured lugging coal trains, here the 7622 powers a mixed freight. EM-1's were used regularly in this type of service on the Cumberland Division's East End.

Railroad Avenue Enterprises

This beautiful image from a low angle is good enough to be a publicity photo. It was taken in 1957, after the locomotive's number had been changed from 7607 to 657 in a systemwide plan to free up four-digit numbers for diesels. Her clean, well-maintained appearance even in her last days was a contrast to late steam on other railroads, which didn't look good in its waning years.

TLC Publishing Inc. Collection

this photo reveals that whatever angle the photographer shoots from, an EM-1 makes an impressive subject. Here, the 7626 crosses a scenic bridge on Sept. 5, 1952.

Bruce D. Fales/Jay Williams Collection

EM-1's often were seen doubleheading, as in this photo of two of the giants on the Sterling-Lorain, Ohio, branch during their later years.

TLC Publishing Inc. Collection

For comparison purposes, here are examples of B&O's earlier articulated models. Class EL-1a 7106 and class EL-2a 7213, seen descending Cranberry Grade west of Terra Alta, W.Va., on June 10, 1949, had come to B&O as 2-8-8-0 compounds, but between 1927 and 1942 were converted to simple operation. A single EM-1 could essentially replace two of these locomotives.

Walter H. Thrall/TLC Publishing Inc. Collection

The 7204, seen here on Salt Lick Curve west of Terra Alta on the same day, is another example of B&O's EL-2a simple 2-8-8-0's. Two pushers are on the rear, out of sight. B&O was not famous for its articulated locomotives — even though it pioneered the type in America — but the sturdy Mallets did well on the company's stiff Allegheny grades.

Walter H. Thrall/TLC Publishing Inc. Collection

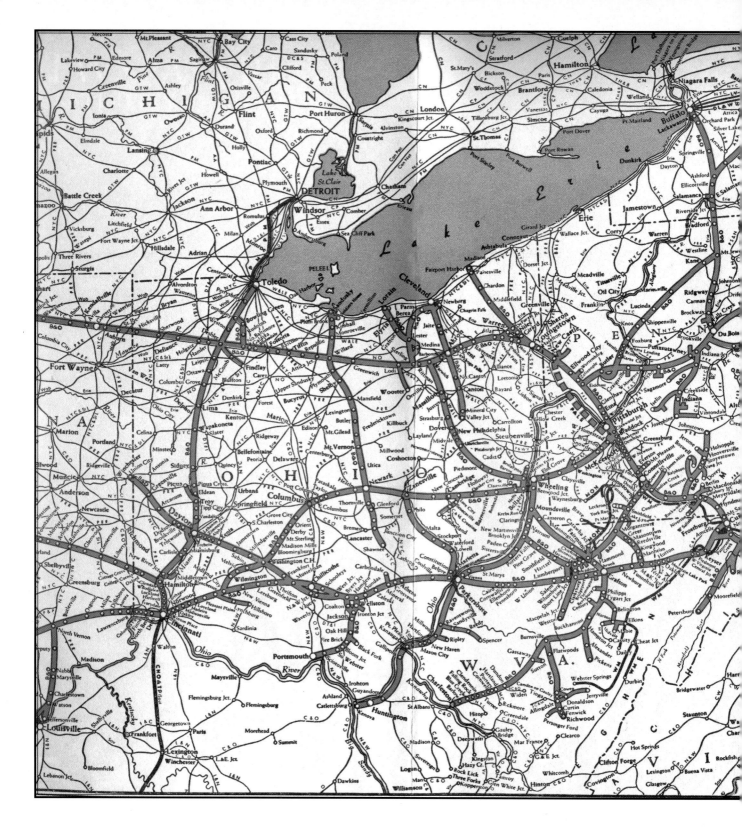

Territories in which the EM-1's operated are shown on this B&O company map. In the following sections, photographs are arranged roughly east-to-west geographically.

TLC Publishing Inc. Collection

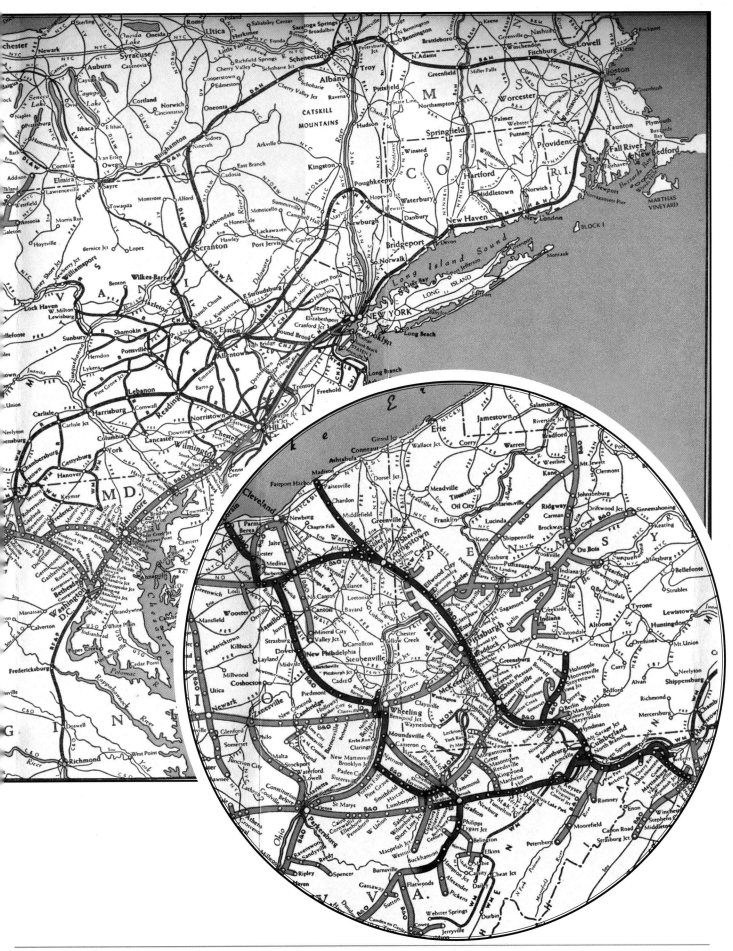

Section Two:
THE CUMBERLAND DIVISION

Although the EM-1's were built expressly for the stiff grades on the Cumberland Division's West End, they were used on the entire division, between Weverton, Md. — actually, Brunswick, Md., three miles east of Weverton on the Baltimore Division — Cumberland, Md., Keyser, W.Va., and Grafton, W.Va., during their earliest years.

The division crossed the state line between Maryland and West Virginia no fewer than seven times, generally following the Potomac River and its North Branch on a fairly level profile most of the way. A single EM-1 initially was rated to pull 4,500 tons westbound from Brunswick to Keyser (via the Patterson Creek Cutoff, which bypassed Cumberland).

B&O faced challenges on the division's 101.4-mile West End with regard to both eastbound and westbound traffic — but most acutely with its huge eastbound coal traffic that had to negotiate four brutal grades, the stiffest Allegheny crossing of any Class 1 railroad. In this territory, westbound EM-1's without helpers were rated for only 1,500 tons.

Those westbound trains departing Keyser had a relatively easy 0.5 percent climb to Piedmont, W.Va., then tackled the Seventeen Mile Grade to the Allegheny summit of 2,628 feet at Altamont, Md., which averaged 2.18 percent and at times reached 2.29 percent. Then they descended a 1.04 percent grade for 6.2 miles to Mountain Lake Park, Md., followed by a roller-coaster profile through a forested plateau called "The Glades" and the city of Oakland, Md., finally climbing up to Terra Alta, W.Va.

From there, they went down the 2.67 percent Cranberry Grade for 11.9 miles to Rowlesburg, W.Va., and back up the 2.06 percent Cheat River Grade to Tunnelton. Once they passed through the Kingwood Tunnel, they started down the 2.28 per-cent Newburg Grade for 7.8 miles to Hardman, located 10 miles east of Grafton.

It was over this jagged terrain that B&O had to haul its freight in both directions. Moreover, the carrier's heaviest trains — eastbound coal mined in the West Virginia fields and assembled in the yards at Fairmont and Grafton — were forced to mount two successive opposing grades of 2.28 percent and 2.67 percent, then make a long descent on a gradient of between 2.18 and 2.29 percent. A tough assignment, indeed.

But the EM-1's made a dramatic difference.

In 1944, the year EM-1's started arriving, eastbound coal traversing those grades amounted to about 60 million tons. In 1945, once the earliest 7600s were added to the motive power mix, B&O increased the average tonnage of eastbound coal trains from 2,700 tons to 2,950 tons and westbound mixed freights from 4,500 tons to 4,650 tons. The overall average engine load for all locomotives on the Cumberland Division's West End increased from 1,339 tons in August 1943 to 1,526 tons in August 1945. In September, a gross trainload record of 2,868 tons was set. Although those figures seem relatively small, they allowed the railroad to increase efficiency remarkably by being able to operate fewer trains over time. The EM-1's proved themselves to be extremely effective in this heavy work, exhibiting a large reserve of power owing to their weight and large fireboxes and boilers.

In addition, since the 7600s arrived during the peak of wartime service and continued until after the end of the conflict, they sometimes were pressed into passenger train service — including regularly scheduled passenger-carrying trains, mail and express runs and heavy troop trains. They often were found lugging up to 18 cars on mail and express train 29 from Cumberland to Grafton — at least until January 21, 1947, when the 7625 derailed, rolled over and killed her engineer just west of Oakland. The engine was rerailed and repaired, but neither she nor her sisters ever handled No. 29 again.

For a while, though, the change had worked well. Previously, No. 29 had been powered by a heavy Pacific with two helpers — a 2-8-2 head-end helper from Piedmont to Blaser, W.Va., and a 2-10-2 rear-end helper from M&K Junction to Blaser. So, on this single operation, the EM-1 eliminated the need for two helper engines and crews.

EM-1's also replaced smaller locomotives on No. 12, the eastbound *Metropolitan Special*, deftly handling up to 14 cars in this territory. Beforehand, a single Pacific had served as the road engine, with a 2-8-2 head-end helper running from Grafton and another 2-8-2 shoving from M&K Junction, both being cut off at Terra Alta. Again, the EM-1 eliminated two locomotives and helper crews.

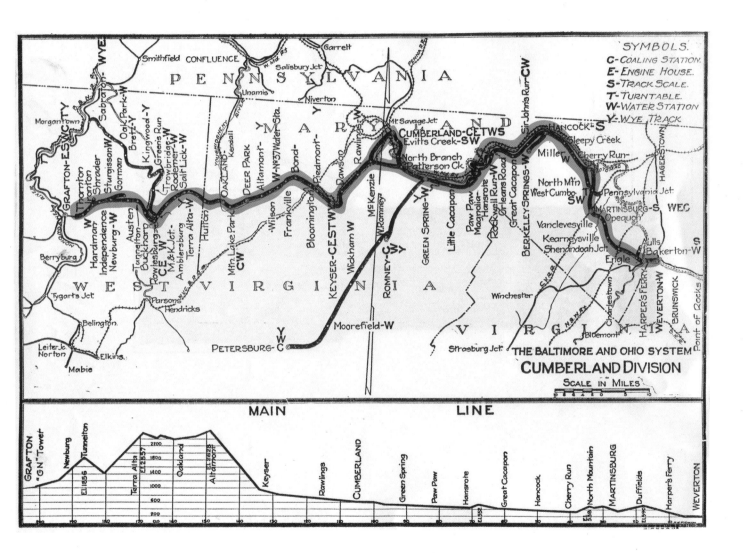

This map, taken from a Cumberland Division employees' timetable, shows the areas on that division in which EM-1's were authorized to operate and a profile that illustrates, more than anything else, B&O's motive power challenges.

TLC Publishing Inc. Collection

EM-1 7614 is at the head end of a westbound mixed freight that's about to depart Weverton in this undated photo. Such assignments were at one time an everyday occurance for the massive Yellowstones.

TLC Publishing Inc. Collection

Engine 7619 offers a grand show of exhaust as it powers a hotshot B&O freight. Note the cut of refrigerator cars right behind the locomotive. In the days before refrigerated trucks, good roads and cheap air freight, railroads handled a lot of perishable meat, vegetables and fruit. Trains carrying the "reefers" were usually the fastest freight on the road. The EM-1's, with their ability to deliver high horsepower at speed, were ideal for that job.

Railroad Avenue Enterprises

These views show EM-1's entering and exiting the Harpers Ferry Tunnel in Maryland, across the Potomac River from the West Virginia town of the same name. Engine 7624 roars out of the tunnel and onto the bridge with empty hoppers bound for coal mines to the West at 9:23 a.m. May 21, 1950, and No. 94 engine 7622 heads eastward into the bore at 1:20 that afternoon.

Bruce D. Fales/Jay Williams Collection

Here are two images of westbound EM-1's racing across the Potomac River Bridge from Maryland into West Virginia at Harpers Ferry. The 7620 is forwarding a section of Timesaver freight 97, with sensitive shipments bound for St. Louis, on Sept. 24, 1946. Neither the other locomotive, its train nor the photo are identified or dated. The EM-1's generous steaming capacity, 64-inch drivers and large tender (note the sweat on the 7620's tender) made them ideal for the demands of B&O's fastest manifest time freights. As usual on such fast trains, loaded refrigerator cars — carrying the most sensitive cargoes of all — are placed right behind the locomotives so they can be periodically cut out at terminals and taken to re-icing stations to assure proper temperature control.

TLC Publishing Inc. Collection

This time, the 7613 is advancing First 97 through Old House Curve, east of Martinsburg, W.Va., at 4 p.m. July 2, 1946.

Bruce D. Fales/Jay Williams Collection

A section of hot-shot manifest No. 94, with the 7627 in command, rolls eastward at Big Pool Junction, Md., on the Western Maryland Railway at 3 p.m. Sept. 20, 1951. The spot is just across the Potomac River from a WM/B&O connection at Cherry Run, W.Va. For several years, B&O ran trains laden with freight for several northeastern U.S. points from Cherry Run to Hagerstown, Md.

Bruce D. Fales/Jay Williams Collection

Sir John's Run, W.Va., figures in several B&O publicity photos, including this one. Westbound EM-1 7618 is passing another train headed by EMD F-units — the wave of the future.

Bruce D. Fales/Jay Williams Collection

Sir John's Run also attracted amateur rail photographers. Engine 7610 urges along a train of empties and engine 7624 is in charge of a 59-car mixed freight. Note how the sunlight highlights various parts of the locomotives.

Bruce D. Fales/Jay Williams Collection

Engine 7616 is captured east of Great Cacapon, W.Va., with Tidewater coal on July 7, 1951.

Bruce D. Fales/Jay Williams Collection

Engine 7616 roars past Great Cacapon's mail crane with a Timesaver freight on Sept. 4, 1952.

Bruce D. Fales/Jay Williams Collection

The 7618 is having an easy time of it with 21 cars of westbound mixed freight on the Magnolia Cutoff. The photographer's excellent elevated angle offers a somewhat rare view of the boiler top.

Bruce D. Fales/Jay Williams Collection

EM-1 7600 forwards more coal toward the Atlantic at Rockwell Run, W.Va., a water stop near the eastern end of the Magnolia Cutoff, at 5:06 p.m. Sept. 11, 1952. B&O opened the cutoff in 1914 to provide a fast, straighter and more elevated two-track main line bypass around several miles of older double track that followed every twist and turn of the Potomac River. Both routes remained in service for years; in this picture, the left two tracks are the cutoff's; the low line's tracks (the northernmost one is not shown) are at right.

Bruce D. Fales/Jay Williams Collection

A photographer, having captured his image, still gazes at the sight. Not one, but two EM-1's, 7617 and 7625, are rumbling above the old line on the Magnolia Cutoff's Magnolia Bridge at — where else? — Magnolia, W.Va., on Oct. 9, 1952.

Bruce D. Fales/Jay Williams Collection

The Magnolia Cutoff is indeed busy on May 27, 1951. The 7607 charges out of Graham Tunnel and across Kessler Bridge with westbound empties at 11:31 a.m., and not long after, here come the 7615 and the 7612 on a manifest. During the time the trains were in the tunnel, they were in Maryland; before they entered and after they exited, they were in West Virginia.

Bruce D. Fales/Jay Williams Collection

No. 94 engine 7620, with the customary complement of refrigerator cars behind the engine, has just entered the west end of the Magnolia Cutoff at Okonoko, W.Va. It's 2:05 p.m. May 27, 1951.

Bruce D. Fales/Jay Williams Collection

On Feb. 19, 1950, the photographer rode a fantrip from Washington D.C., to Cumberland, where he captured several poses of EM-1's on this and other occasions. Shown in these views are engines 7613 (with Class S-1 2-10-2 6110), 7619, 7629, 7611 and 7626.

Bruce D. Fales/Jay Williams Collection

Engine 7600 departs for Grafton from Viaduct Junction in Cumberland with a westbound mixed freight. B&O's line to Chicago diverges behind the tower visible above the tender and boxcar.

Railroad Avenue Enterprises

Here are several images of EM-1's in Keyser's shop and yard — seen are the 7600, 7606, 7608, 7615 and 7616. Keyser was located at the eastern base of the Seventeen Mile Grade, which afforded a severe challenge to B&O even though most of its eastbound coal traffic from West Virginia moved downward on that hill. Note the engines' details — the 7606's trailing truck and the bottom of her tender are white from sand blowing up off the drivers during mountain climbs, the difference between inside and outside temperatures makes the lower half of 7608's tender sweat, and the view of the 7615 clearly shows the locomotives' double-stack exhaust.

TLC Publishing Inc. and Jay Williams Collections

Westbound with empty hoppers, the 7621 is running west of Keyser with a clean stack.

Bruce D. Fales/Jay Williams Collection

Standing at Piedmont in these two photos is the 7603 with westbound empties. Momentarily, Class S-1 2-10-2 6108, pulling duty as a helper on the Seventeen Mile Grade, pulls up alongside to lend a hand.

Railroad Avenue Enterprises

There is no visible exhaust from the 7614's stack, but plenty of smoke from the hot brake shoes of 52 loads of coal is evident as the eastbound coal train trundles between Bloomington, Md., and Piedmont, W.Va., at the foot of Seventeen Mile Grade on June 12, 1949.

Bruce D. Fales/Jay Williams Collection

Three sources provide these next six views of EM-1's in the vicinity of Altamont, at the 2,628-foot crest of the Seventeen Mile Grade. The 7608 approaches from the East; No. 96 engine 7614 is negotiating the curve just east of AM Tower on June 12, 1949; the 7603 brings an eastbound 50-car drag by the tower's windows on May 28, 1950; the 7605 and the 7629 proceed west beyond the tower; and the 7627 approaches the tower from the West on May 28, 1950. Note the distinctive B&O wagon-top boxcar near the head end.

Railroad Enterprises, Bruce D. Fales/Jay Williams Collection, TLC Publishing Inc. Collection

(Caption on Page 25)

Finally on level track after cresting Cranberry Grade, engine 7614 heads toward Tidewater with 55 loads of coal east of Terra Alta, W.Va., at 11:02 a.m. May 28, 1950.

Bruce D. Fales/Jay Williams Collection

Engine 7614, beautifully backlighted, approaches Terra Alta from the East with 82 cars at 12:05 p.m. Nov. 14, 1948.

TLC Publishing Inc. Collection

Engine 7619 wheels an eastbound stock train past the water plug at Terra Alta at 8:11 a.m. March 25, 1945.

TLC Publishing Inc. Collection

Engine 7627 and a train of empties crosses over to the center of three main tracks in downtown Terra Alta

Railroad Avenue Enterprises

Engine 7618 soils any white sheets that may be hanging on nearby clotheslines as she rolls through Terra Alta in June 1944.

TLC Publishing Inc. Collection

Engine 7604, serving on pusher duty, rests between trains at Terra Alta, top of the Cranberry Grade, in June 1944.

TLC Publishing Inc. Collection

Engine 7613 and 80 westbound empties rumble through Terra Alta, heading toward West Virginia coal mines on Oct. 19, 1947.

Bruce D. Fales/Jay Williams Collection

Engine 7606 starts down Cranberry Grade at Terra Alta in
June 1944.

TLC Publishing Inc. Collection

The engineer of No. 7611
eases off on the throttle as
his heavy eastbound coal
drag crests the summit of
Cranberry Grade at Terra
Alta on May 28, 1950.

*Bruce D. Fales/Jay Wil-
liams Collection*

In a few moments, the 7618
can breathe a little easier as
she successfully brings the
rest of her train over the crest
of the Cranberry Grade at Terra Alta in this undated photo.

TLC Publishing Inc. Collection

One can plainly see the crest of Cranberry Grade at Terra Alta as engine 7614 starts downhill on May 28, 1950, with a train of empties.

Bruce D. Fales/Jay Williams Collection

A little farther to the West, engine 7612 has departed Terra Alta, returning more empties to the West Virginia mines on June 18, 1950.

Bruce D. Fales/Jay Williams Collection

Remarkably with a clean stack, engine 7619 strives to lug a 52-car coal drag up Cranberry Grade west of Terra Alta on June 12, 1949.

Bruce D. Fales/Jay Williams Collection

Engine 7629 eases down Cranberry Grade west of Terra Alta with 58 empties at 10:25 a.m. May 28, 1950. We know that B&O's Everett L. "Tommy" Thompson was with the photographer that day. Could that be him standing in the distance on the eastbound main?

Bruce D. Fales/Jay Williams Collection

In these two photos, 2-8-8-0's 7109 (Class EL-1a) and 7202 (Class EL-2), both built by Baldwin in 1916, shove Extra 7169 East around Salt Lick Curve west of Terra Alta at 11:26 a.m. June 12, 1949. These older Mallets were eventually replaced by the war-baby EM-1's.

Bruce D. Fales/Jay Williams Collection

Engine 7602 lifts an eastbound coal drag around Salt Lick Curve west of Terra Alta.

Bruce D. Fales/Jay Williams Collection

Two more views, undated, show the 7613 and the 7622 eastbound, in the same vicinity.

TLC Publishing Inc. Collection

Engine 7610 brings an eastbound 52-car coal drag around Salt Lick Curve west of Terra Alta on May 28, 1950.

Bruce D. Fales/Jay Williams Collection

Engine 7613 and a train of empties drift down Cranberry Grade approaching McGuire Tunnel Cut west of Terra Alta in March 1945.

Bruce D. Fales/Jay Williams Collection

Engine 7614 brings 82 empties through McGuire Tunnel Cut west of Terra Alta at 12:28 p.m. Nov. 14, 1948.

Bruce D. Fales/Jay Williams Collection

Engine 7624, hauling 52 loads of eastbound coal up Cranberry Grade, blasts under a signal bridge at Rodemer, W.Va., at 1:07 p.m. Sept. 28, 1948. Anyone standing on the signal bridge above the beast will have to bathe thoroughly tonight.

Bruce D. Fales/Jay Williams Collection

Engine 7612 struggles up Cranberry Grade east of Amblersburg, W.Va., with eastbound "Quick Dispatch" freight train 96 at 3:53 p.m. on June 11, 1949. Two more Mallets are shoving on the rear end.

Walter H. Thrall

The same train is seen — a few seconds later, and a few feet higher. Could that be Walter Thrall standing by the westbound main?

Bruce D. Fales/Jay Williams Collection

The 7622's engineer has his iron horse exerting all of her 115,000 pounds of tractive effort hauling an eastbound mixed freight up Cranberry Grade near Amblersburg circa 1947.

Bruce D. Fales/Jay Williams Collection

Several refrigerated loads of Midwestern produce head up Train 96 as engine 7616 works up Cranberry Grade at 3:40 p.m. Sept. 28, 1948.

Bruce D. Fales/Jay Williams Collection

Engine 7600, B&O's original Class EM-1 2-8-8-4, drifts down Cranberry Grade with a train of empties in June 1949.

Bruce D. Fales/Jay Williams Collection

Engine 7623 rounds a curve on Cranberry Grade with a train of empties at 11:50 a.m. June 10, 1949.

Bruce D. Fales/Jay Williams Collection

Engine 7605 drifts through McMillan, W.Va., at the east end of Rowlesburg, with empty hoppers in June 1949.

Bruce D. Fales/Jay Williams Collection

An unidentified EM-1 eases through McMillan, at the bottom of Cranberry Grade, with yet another train of empties, on June 11, 1949.

Bruce D. Fales/Jay Williams Collection

Engine 7606, tended by a talented fireman who produces white smoke, rumbles through M&K Junction at Rowlesburg with a coal train in June 1944.

TLC Publishing Inc. Collection

Engine 7605 rattles the windows of R Tower at M&K Junction (just out of the photo) in Rowlesburg with westbound empties at 5:15 p.m. Sept. 28, 1948. The tower, which routed helpers returning to M&K from their shoves on Newburg, Cheat and Cranberry grades, housed 68 levers and required three men to operate them.

Bruce D. Fales/Jay Williams Collection

Engine 7624 begins its ascent up Cheat River Grade at Rowlesburg at 5:31 on the foggy morning of June 11, 1949. We suspect that the photographer has just spent the night at Annette Howard's noted trackside hotel, visible at left. If you got the right room, you would be tempted to watch trains in your sleep!

Bruce D. Fales/Jay Williams Collection

Engine 7622 charges up Cheat River Grade with westbound empties on July 26, 1949.

R.H. Kindig

The 7627, just three months old and running against the current of traffic, ascends the Cheat River Grade west of Rowlesburg with mail and express train 29 on October 21, 1945.

E.L. Thompson/B&O Historical Society Collection

No. 96 engine 7610, traveling at 30 miles an hour, rumbles past K Tower at Blaser, W.Va., on Oct. 16, 1947.

Bruce D. Fales/Jay Williams Collection

Engine 7619 lugs a coal drag under the North Street pedestrian overpass at Tunnelton, W.Va. It's 10:32 a.m. on June 11, 1949.

Bruce D. Fales/Jay Williams Collection

It's 10:20 a.m. on the same day, and engine 7620 approaches Tunnelton with an earlier coal train. The drag has just exited the double-tracked "new" (1912) Kingwood Tunnel through Laurel Mountain; the line leading to the old bore — which offered no end of trouble from the time it was built in the 1850s until it was taken out of service in 1956 — can be seen on the bank above the train.

Bruce D. Fales/Jay Williams Collection

Engine 7607, hauling westbound empties, prepares to enter the old Kingwood Tunnel in 1949. The old line was about 24 feet higher than the double-tracked line leading to the new bore, seen at bottom right.

Bruce D. Fales/Jay Williams Collection

No. 96 engine 7618, running against the current of traffic on the westbound main, emerges from the new Kingwood Tunnel at Tunnelton at 11:53 a.m. June 11, 1949. The train has completed its trip up Newburg Grade and now will start down the Cheat River Grade toward Rowlesburg.

Bruce D. Fales/Jay Williams Collection

Twenty-two minutes later on the same westbound main, engine 7610 with what appears to be loads of ore or gravel prepares to enter the New Kingwood Tunnel en route to Grafton.

Bruce D. Fales/Jay Williams Collection

Engine 7620 and an eastbound trainload of coal prepare to enter the new Kingwood Tunnel at West End, W.Va., which is located across Laurel Mountain from Tunnelton. The postcard upon which is photo is shown was mailed by noted railroad photographer William Price to Robert Hunt, the freight and ticket agent at Tunnelton, in December 1948.

Herbert Brown

No. 96 engine 7609, with 49 cars, approaches West End's WS Tower at 11:25 a.m. Oct. 18, 1947. The Kingwood Tunnels are just ahead.

Bruce D. Fales/Jay Williams Collection

Fourteen minutes later, engine 7608 hauls 54 cars of coal past nearly the same spot.

Bruce D. Fales/Jay Williams Collection

Engine 7611 hauls 51 loads of coal past West End at 1:15 p.m. June 10, 1949. The exhaust of two helpers can be seen in the distance.

Bruce D. Fales/Jay Williams Collection

These two photos show an eastbound 54-car coal train at Austen, W.Va., on the Newburg Grade at 5:48 p.m. July 27, 1949. EM-1 7609 on the point, assisted by two pushers on the rear — one of which is Class EL-3a 2-8-8-0 7133.

Bruce D. Fales/Jay Williams Collection

Engine 7629 lugs more eastbound coal by Austen on the Newburg Grade on July 27, 1949.

Bruce D. Fales/Jay Williams Collection

Section Three:
THE DIESEL-DRIVEN DISPERSAL

When B&O first sent 28 F-7's to the Cumberland Division's West End in 1949, they were reclassified as DH-1 and assigned to helper duty. That dispatched the EM-1's from the territory for which they were built to other climes, principally to the Pittsburgh Division, running northwestwardly on the Baltimore-Chicago route between Cumberland and New Castle, Pa., (including the famous Sand Patch Grade, which crested the Allegheny Mountains at 2,258 feet) and a branch between Rockwood and Johnstown, Pa.; the Monongah and Wheeling divisions from Fairmont, W.Va., through Brooklyn Junction and Benwood Junction, W.Va., to Holloway and Lorain, Ohio, to haul Mountain State coal to Lake Erie docks; and the Akron Division's Lake Branch to Fairport Harbor, Ohio, hauling more Lake coal north (timetable east) and — in season — heavy ore trains on the backhaul bound for Youngstown, Ohio, steel mills. The following section features photographs taken in those areas.

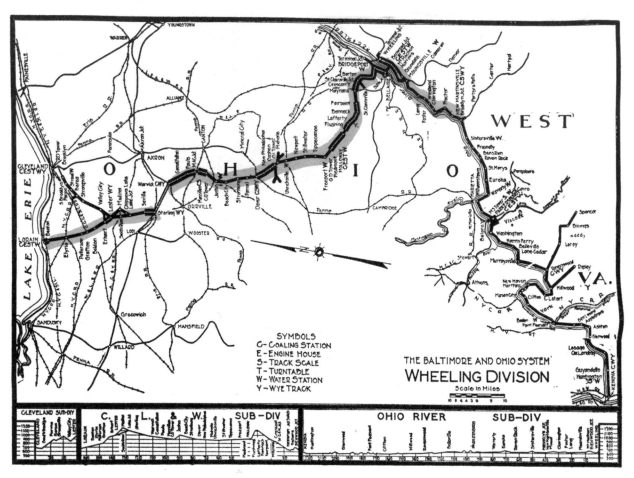

This map, taken from a Wheeling Division employees' timetable, shows the areas on that division in which EM-1's were authorized to operate and their profiles.

TLC Publishing Inc. Collection

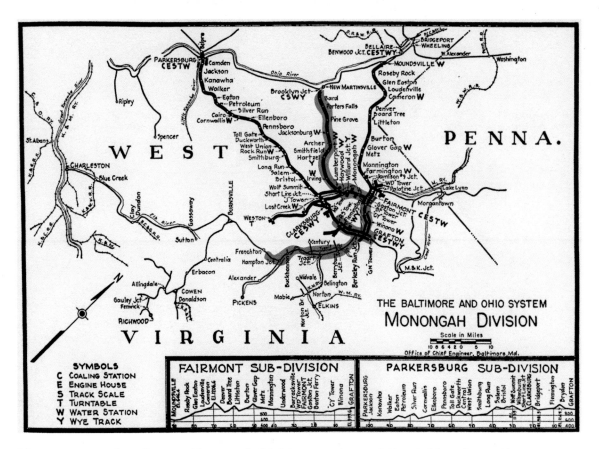

These maps, taken from a Monongah Division employees' timetable, shows the areas on that division in which EM-1's were authorized to operate and their profiles.

TLC Publishing Inc. Collection

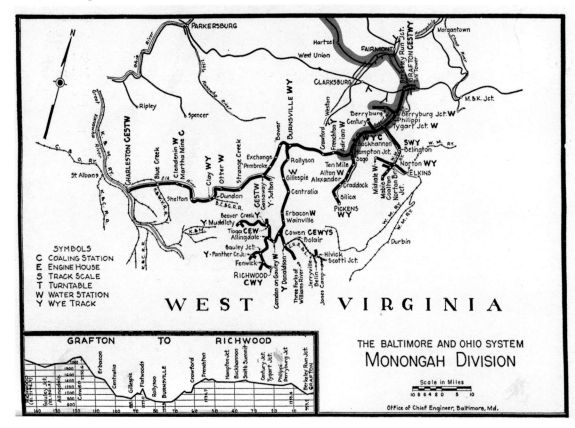

Engine 651, with Road Foreman of Engines A.K. Jacobs leaning out of the gangway, waits on the eastbound main at SW Tower in McMechen, W.Va., in August 1957 as sister 670 crosses over to the westbound main with a coal train from Fairmont bound for the yard at Benwood Junction.

J.J. Young Jr./Bob Withers Collection

With Extra 670 East out of the way, the 651 and its "Fairmonter" highballs away from SW Tower as the rain gets heavier.

J.J. Young Jr./Bob Withers Collection

Engines 672 and 677 show off their massive dimensions even as they snooze in the roundhouse at Benwood Junction in the summer of 1957.

Charles W. Aurand/Bob Withers Collection

Its exquisite detail appearing to shine, the 666 — truly, the number is the mark of a beast — slumbers in the Benwood Junction roundhouse on Sept. 25, 1957.

Bruce D. Fales/Jay Williams Collection

Engines 650, 676 and an unidentified sister rest between runs at the Benwood Junction shop in August 1957. The little sign, barely visible at left, says "Open cylinder cocks before moving or leaving engines."

J.J. Young Jr./Bob Withers Collection

Engine 7608 simmers beside a water plug at the Benwood shop in July 1956.

Joe Schmitz

Engine 7608 simmers beside a water plug at the Benwood shop in July 1956.

Joe Schmitz

A Benwood shop employee fills the 7627's front sand box in July 1956.

Joe Schmitz

Engine 670 takes a ride on the turntable at Benwood Junction on Sept. 25, 1957, and, a few minutes later, enjoys a sunbath on the crisp fall afternoon. Soon, but not for much longer, she will take yet another Holloway humper out of town.

Bruce D. Fales/Jay Williams Collection

EM-1 675 is ready to depart Benwood Junction in the summer of 1957.

TLC Publishing Inc. Collection

It's 9:40 on a warm summer morning in August 1956, and the photographer has been blessed with a lucky moment. A bridge and building gang has delayed EM-1 7607, which is coupled to a train-load of coal bound for Holloway, on the approach to the Ohio River bridge be-tween Benwood Junction, W.Va., and Bellaire, Ohio. In the background, P-7 Pacific 5300 is departing Benwood's station with passenger train 430 on the last lap of its Grafton-Wheeling run. Still farther in the background, GP-9 680 waits on a "loop" track with a long string of empties for two Valley Camp Coal Company mines at Elm Grove, W.Va. The loop was built so Wheeling-bound trains coming off the bridge and heading south could easily reverse di-rection and continue northward.

J.J. Young Jr./Bob Withers collection

The 7626, toting a string of empties, passes the Benwood Junction station as she brings her train off the Benwood-Bel-laire bridge. The photo is undated, but it's obviously a cold winter day.

TLC Publishing Inc. Collection

Engine 657 approaches the West Virginia side of the Benwood-Bellaire bridge in the summer of 1957.

TLC Publishing Inc. Collection

An EM-1 crosses the Ohio River after departing Benwood Junction with a trainload of Lake-bound coal in March 1954. These drags were called "humpers" after B&O's sawtooth profile between that point and Holloway, Ohio.

J.J. Young Jr./Bob Withers Collection

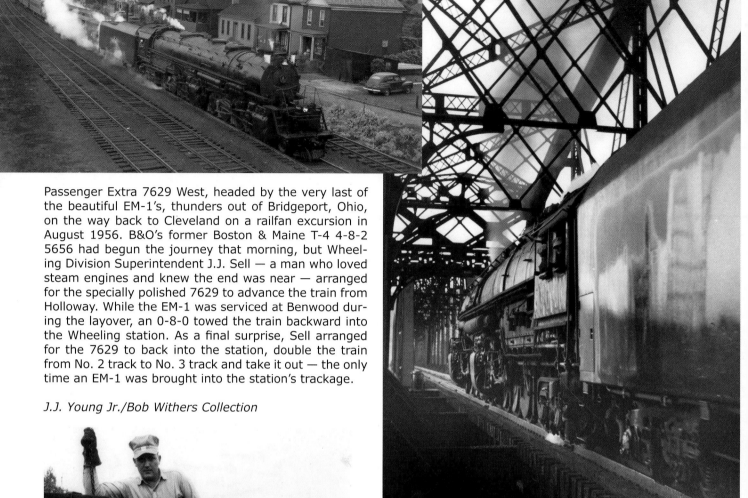

Passenger Extra 7629 West, headed by the very last of the beautiful EM-1's, thunders out of Bridgeport, Ohio, on the way back to Cleveland on a railfan excursion in August 1956. B&O's former Boston & Maine T-4 4-8-2 5656 had begun the journey that morning, but Wheeling Division Superintendent J.J. Sell — a man who loved steam engines and knew the end was near — arranged for the specially polished 7629 to advance the train from Holloway. While the EM-1 was serviced at Benwood during the layover, an 0-8-0 towed the train backward into the Wheeling station. As a final surprise, Sell arranged for the 7629 to back into the station, double the train from No. 2 track to No. 3 track and take it out — the only time an EM-1 was brought into the station's trackage.

J.J. Young Jr./Bob Withers Collection

The photographer has walked out to a fire barrel platform to catch this close-up of engine 7607 on the Benwood-Bellaire bridge as it pulls a humper out of Benwood in September 1955.

J.J. Young Jr./Bob Withers Collection

Fireman Harry Greenwood tops off EM-1 7618's water tank near the Lincoln Avenue crossing in Bridgeport — his last chance before the humper starts climbing a 26-mile hill to Flushing, Ohio — in October 1954.

J.J. Young Jr./Bob Withers Collection

Greenwood's engineer, John "Silver Fox" Kettlewell, urges the 7618 up the hill at Lansing, Ohio, four miles beyond Bridgeport.

J.J. Young Jr./Bob Withers Collection

EM-1 No. 657 has satisfied her thirst in Bridgeport and is making headway toward Holloway in the summer of 1957 in these three views.

TLC Publishing Inc. Collection

A little while later, on the same day, the 657 and her train prepare to enter Barton Tunnel.

Don Wood/TLC Publishing Inc. Collection

B&O engineer Prestley Hill checks the water glass in the cab of the 657 in summer 1957 as his Holloway humper charges through Apple Hill, Ohio, west of Barton.

J.J. Young Jr./Bob Withers Collection

From a distance, the photographer catches the 671 southbound near Lafferty, Ohio, on May 13, 1957.

TLC Publishing Inc. Collection

Engine 657 breaks out of Flushing Tunnel, cresting the long climb and entering the town of the same name, on July 16, 1957.

John A. Rehor

These views show EM-1's near Holloway advancing empties toward West Virginia mines. An unidentified engine works on June 4, 1955, and the 7616 hurries along on the following July 5.

Railroad Avenue Enterprises/TLC Publishing Inc. Collection

Engine 671 is being prepared for another run out of Holloway on July 15, 1957.

John A. Rehor

Westbound engine 7614 hauls 116 carloads of mixed freight through Justus, Ohio, on July 5, 1955.

Railroad Avenue Enterprises

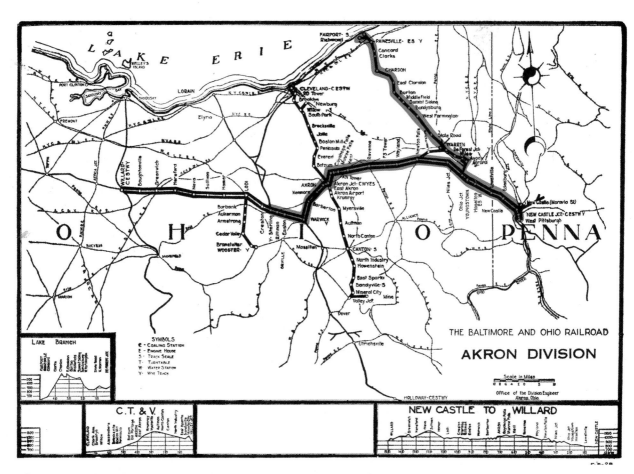

This map, taken from an Akron Division employees' timetable, shows the areas on that division in which EM-1's were authorized to operate and their profiles.

TLC Publishing Inc. Collection

Engine 7610 departs the coal dock at Warwick, Ohio, on July 17, 1956, with a trainload of coal for Lorain. The next 11.9 miles of track, between Warwick and Sterling, Ohio, belonged to the Akron Division (part of the route of B&O's New York-Baltimore-Chicago passenger trains), and connected two separated sections of the Wheeling Division.

TLC Publishing Inc. Collection

An unidentified EM-1 forwards a coal drag between Warwick and Sterling on May 29, 1956, en route to Lorain.

TLC Publishing Inc. Collection

Engine 678, en route from Holloway to Lorain, has traversed the short section of B&O's Akron Division and now is returning to Wheeling Division rails at Sterling, in June 1957.

TLC Publishing Inc. Collection

On another day, the 678 charges northbound between Sterling and Seville, Ohio.

TLC Publishing Inc. Collection

The coal behind engine 678 is nearing its destination in Lorain as the EM-1 hauls it along Railroad Street in Seville on Aug. 25, 1957.

TLC Publishing Inc. Collection

Engine 679 has a string of empties well in hand as she chugs toward Holloway on a high bank south of Lester, Ohio, on Sept. 18, 1957.

TLC Publishing Inc. Collection

These next seven photos provide an interesting study of engine 672 during a water stop at Lester on June 13, 1957. First, she has been uncoupled from her train and slakes her thirst at the water plug. While she does that, a railroad employee works on the front sandbox while the photographer captures several crisp views of her running gear. Finally, with her train reattached, she departs for Lorain and passes a small lake just out of town. It must be a hot day — see how the tender, now full of cold, sloshing water, is sweating? (See following page)

TLC Publishing Inc. Collection

Engine 7614 is ready to depart Lester, eastbound, in the mid-1950s.

Philip T. Horning

Engine 7624 is seen between Lester and Erhart, Ohio, as it forwards coal to Lorain on April 30, 1956.

TLC Publishing Inc. Collection

Class T-3c 4-8-2 5586 is in the hole at Erhart for an eastbound train of empties pulled by EM-1 7613. The Mountain-type locomotive, one of the last built by B&O's Mount Clare Shop in Baltimore, is three years younger than the Baldwin war baby charging past on the main line.

Philip T. Horning

Engine 7624 blackens the sky as it urges a 69-car ore drag eastbound near Erhart on May 19, 1956. Q-3 2-8-2 4508 is assisting, but is so far to the rear, the photographer can't even see her smoke — in either view.

TLC Publishing Inc. Collection

Engine 672, boasting of a crystal clear stack, hurries 123 empties through Beldon, Ohio, on May 31, 1957.

Railroad Avenue Enterprises

Lorain-bound engine 674 crosses the New York Central's Cleveland-Columbus line at Grafton, Ohio, on April 13, 1957.

TLC Publishing Inc. Collection

The 655 steams toward Lorain near Elyria, Ohio, in June 1957.

TLC Publishing Inc. Collection

Engine 660 and an identified sister rest between runs in Lorain on Sept. 19, 1957. The 660 will be laid up permanently in less than two months.

Bruce D. Fales/Jay Williams Collection

The 7600 struggles to keep her belly warm in New Castle, Pa., on a wintry day. She must be doing a good job — the pops are going off.

Bruce D. Fales/Jay Williams Collection

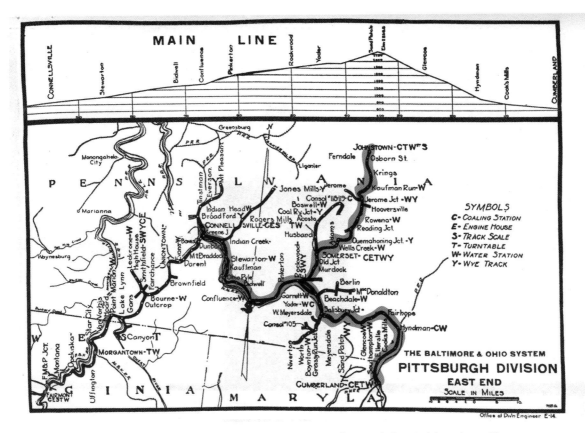

These maps, taken from a Pittsburgh Division employees' timetable, show the areas on that division in which EM-1's were authorized to operate and their profiles.

TLC Publishing Inc. Collection

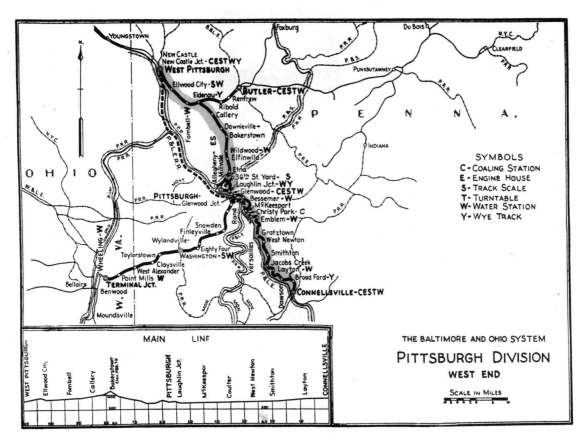

The photographer captures three EM-1's in New Castle during 1956 — the 7614 in February, the 7600 in May, and the 7617 in October.

Joe Schmitz

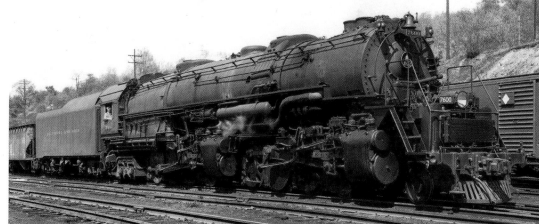

It's the final year for steam, and more photographers flock to New Castle. Seen here are the 7610 (she will be renumbered 660 in March), the 657 and the 673.

Bruce D. Fales/Jay Williams Collection

An unidentified EM-1, with some kind of name plate covering her traditional B&O Capitol dome emblem, leaves Akron, Ohio, headed for Painesville, Ohio, on a fantrip in this undated photo.

TLC Publishing Inc. Collection

This is a going-away shot of the fantrip pictured at the bottom of page 63.

TLC Publishing Inc. Collection

In July 1956, engine 7603 waits in the Failes, Ohio, spur, with derail in place, for her turn to assist a coal train.

John Rehor/Jay Williams Collection

These two views show double-headed EM-1's hauling coal through the West Farmington, Ohio, area on the Failes-Chardon helper district, in 1956. In the first image, the locomotives are unidentified. In the second, number plates reveal the 7629 and the 7602.

TLC Publishing Inc. Collection

These three views show a Fairport Harbor-bound coal drag headed by EM-1 7609 picking up a head-end helper — which has backed down from Painesville — at Failes, Ohio, on July 19, 1956, as far as Chardon, 20 miles distant. Two views show the drag arriving — as well as a friendly helper crew — and the third shows the train, now doubleheaded, departing.

TLC Publishing Inc. Collection

Southbound trains of empties needed no helper between Chardon and Failes. Here, engine 7617 totes another long string of them through West Farmington. They will probably return in a few days, loaded with more coal for the Lake Erie docks at Fairport Harbor.

TLC Publishing Inc. Collection

These views show EM-1's charging through Middlefield, Ohio, in 1956 — the 7617 on May 5 and the 7603, with an unidentified sister, in June.

TLC Publishing Inc. Collection/Philip T. Horning

Engines 7603 roar through the Chardon, Ohio, area with a coal drag on Sept. 4, 1956.

TLC Publishing Inc. Collection

The 7600 rests between assignments at the engine terminal in Painesville, Ohio, just a stone's throw from the Lake Erie docks at Fairport Harbor.

TLC Publishing Inc. Collection

Section Four:
THEN COMETH THE END

Clouds began to gather in 1956 for the EM-1's — indeed, for all 444 B&O steam locomotives remaining in service — when the company ordered their renumbering into three-digit slots so four-digit series could be applied to the ever-advancing onslaught of diesels. The first hints of gloom actually had taken place when at least two EM-1's, the 7600 and the 7629, were operated on several "farewell to steam" fantrips earlier that year.

The renumbering edict of November 1 ordered locomotive shops all over the system to move the EM-1's from the 7600-7629 slot to the 650-679 series. The new identities, which amounted to in-service death certificates, began appearing in early 1957. It is not certain that all B&O steam locomotives received their new numbers before they were retired, but all 30 of the EM-1's did, as follows:

OLD NUMBER	NEW NUMBER
7600	650
7601	651
7602	652
7603	653
7604	654
7605	655
7606	656
7607	657
7608	658
7609	659
7610	660
7611	661
7612	662
7613	663
7614	664
7615	665
7616	666
7617	667
7618	668
7619	669
7620	670
7621	671
7622	672
7623	673
7624	674
7625	675
7626	676
7627	677
7628	678
7629	679

From that point, the end came quickly. The 661 made her last trip, from Holloway to Lorain, on November 19, 1957. The 662's swan song followed on the 26th, and the 655's on the 29th, both on the same run. The 657 made her last trip, from Holloway to Benwood, on December 10, and the final recorded run of any EM-1 anywhere occurred on a Holloway-Lorain round trip December 23.

William D. Edson's seminal *Steam Locomotives of the Baltimore & Ohio: An All-Time Roster*, self-published in 1992, listed the 652, 654, 663, 664, and 667 as dropped from the company's roster in 1957. The 655, 656, 657, 658, 661, 662 and 669 were listed as scrapped in 1958. The remaining 18, including all 10 that were delivered in 1945, were listed as either scrapped or dropped from the roster in 1960.

But even though Edson listed the 659 as scrapped in 1960, it remained hot well into that year — serving with sister 651 to supply steam heat to Allied Chemical and Dye Corporation's Solvay Process Division plant Perkins, W.Va., 10 miles south of Benwood.

Retired engineers recall that the Solvay service began in 1959. At first, the locomotives were coal-fired in the usual way, but later they were stripped of their tenders and positioned cab-to-cab, with a natural gas line running out from the plant, splitting at a T-joint and running three 2-inch jets through each firedoor. Then the only task of B&O firemen assigned to keep watch was to sit in an old truck beside the cab windows, monitor the water glasses and read magazines. It is said that the old warhorses used more gas than the entire city of Moundsville.

B&O ran what it billed as the last steam run anywhere on the system on May 17, 1958, when Class Q-4 2-8-2 No. 421 powered a fantrip from Cleveland to Holloway and return. But, for whatever reason, that trip really wasn't the last steam run. Class Q-3 2-8-2 No. 314 steamed on the Ohio Division until July 22, 1958, and four 0-8-0's remained in service on the B&O Chicago Terminal until the following November. And remarkably, photographs of the 421 under steam, supplying heat to a Cleveland engine house as late as 1959, were published in *Baltimore & Ohio Trackside with Willis A. McCaleb* (Morning Sun Books, 1998).

Meanwhile, EM-1 659 showed up again, with its tender restored, at Butler Junction, Pa., when it was photographed by Robert E. Rathke on June 15, 1961. Rathke came to suspect that her existence at such a late date meant that she was the locomotive that the railroad meant to save for the B&O Railroad Museum in Baltimore, but because of some bureaucratic snafu along the way, neither it or any other EM-1 survived — which is, of course, a dastardly tragedy.

Others believe it may have been the 679, the last of her class, which was meant to be saved — because company reports show her *inside* the Cumberland shop as late as April 1, 1960. Perhaps no one will know for sure the full story of one of B&O's biggest and saddest mistakes.

In what may be the last photo of an EM-1, the 659 — her firebox last warmed by natural gas instead of coal — rusts away at Butler Junction, Pa., on Thursday, June 15, 1961. Some believe that because the locomotive still exists at such a late date, she is destined for the B&O Railroad Museum. But isn't Butler Junction dangerously close to the Dietz Scrap Company in nearby Aspinwall, where scores of other steam locomotives met their doom? We should be thankful for the photographers who traipsed all over the mountain passes, hills and hollows, and busy rail yards to preserve their too-brief existence for all time.

Robert E. Rathke/Bob Withers collection

COME BLOW YOUR WHISTLE
WITH OURS!

Throughout B & O's territory—the "Heart of Industrial America"—manufacturers are locating their plants. They know that here are vast natural resources, diversified agriculture, unparalleled power, labor, and markets.

These builders of industry frequently call on B & O's Industrial Development Department. This department, experienced in engineering, traffic and plant location, will be glad to weigh YOUR problems in the light of their knowledge of the area served by B & O; then prepare for your consideration studies and surveys evaluating *facts* of interest to your particular industry.

Why not profit by our "know-how" and experience?

WRITE FOR THIS UP-TO-THE-MINUTE DATA

"A LION'S SHARE"—a 54-page brochure covering many aspects of development, including: resources, power, labor, markets and transportation within the B & O area.

NATURAL RESOURCES MAP and DEVELOPMENT MAP—geographically correct, drawn-to-scale maps of Northeastern United States.

Address B & O Industrial Department Representative nearest you:
New York 4, N. Y. • Baltimore 1, Md. • Pittsburgh 22, Pa. • Cincinnati 2, Ohio • Chicago 7, Ill.

BALTIMORE & OHIO RAILROAD

LINKING 13 GREAT STATES WITH THE NATION

A Million-Pound Fighter THAT'S EARNING ITS STRIPES

● To augment the already powerful B&O fleet, giant, new Mallet locomotives have been put into service to rush vital shipments through faster.

Though rail traffic in 1944 is challenging many all-time records for the movement of freight we, of the B&O .. all 70,000 of us . . . are confident that with the added power of our new, million-pound Mallets—plus the continued whole-hearted support of government officials, shippers and receivers of freight, travelers and others whom we serve—the mammoth victory load, entrusted to the B&O, can and will be delivered on time !

R. B. WHITE, President

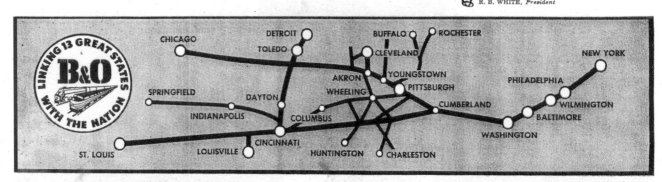

BALTIMORE & OHIO RAILROAD